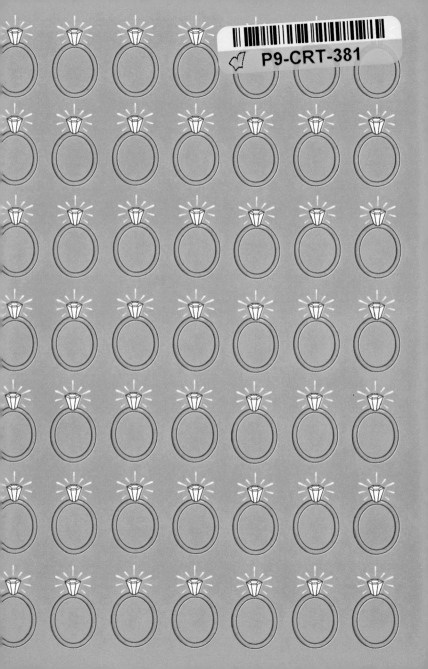

Are You My Husband?

First published in the United States of America in 2003
by UNIVERSE PUBLISHING
A Division of Rizzoli International Publications, Inc.
300 Park Avenue South
New York, NY 10010
www.rizzoliusa.com

© 2003 by Rachel Carpenter

Illustrations by Sarah Bereczki
Design by Annemarie Gilligan

2003 2004 2005 2006 2007/10 9 8 7 6 5 4 3 2 1

Printed in the U.S.A

www.rachelcarpenter.com

Library of Congress Cataloging-in-Publication Data

Carpenter, Rachel.
  Are you my husband? : a parody / by Rachel Carpenter ; illustrations
by Sarah Bereczki.
     p. cm.
Parody of Are you my mother? by P.D. Eastman.
  ISBN 0-7893-0975-0
  1. American wit and humor. 2. Eastman, P. D. (Philip D.)--Parodies,
imitations, etc. I. Bereczki, Sarah. II. Eastman, P. D. (Philip D.).
You my mother? III. Title.
PN6231.P3 C28 2003
813'.6--dc22

                         2003016744

Are You My Husband?

by Rachel Carpenter
Illustrations by Sarah Bereczki

A Parody

Universe

The Little Chick woke up one day and she was thirty.

"Oh my," she said, "I must get a husband. Otherwise, what will happen to my eggs?"

{She was very concerned about her eggs.}

So she got out of bed and went to find a husband.

There were lots of places to meet a husband,
her married friends said.

Most of them wanted her to marry, since that's
what married friends tend to want their
unmarried friends to do.

Some of their own eggs had already hatched.

The Little Chick asked them where she could find a husband.

"Everyone's into ballroom dancing now, Little Chick," one friend said. "Cha cha, foxtrot, waltz, tango—take your pick."

So she did.

But it's hard to dance when you have only three toes.

"*Are you my husband?*" she asked the rooster to her left
when it came time to switch partners. He was stepping on his
partner's feet on every off-beat.

"No, Little Chick, I am not your husband. I am getting married to this chick right here. Can you skip me and go on to the next man, since we need to practice for our wedding?"

So she did.

The Little Chick skipped the next guy, and the next, and the next. All of them were practicing for their weddings.

"One and two and one and two," they all said. The
Little Chick learned to say "one and two" too,
but that was about it.

"Take another kind of class," another married friend suggested. "The kind where you don't have to pair up, like a pottery class or something."

he Little Chick, who was rather literal, took a pottery class.

"Pardon me, Little Chick," the only guy in the class said t
her with a gentle smile. "Is this seat taken?"

That was easy, the Little Chick thought, and smiled back.

"Are you my husband?" she asked,
and his gentle smile vanished.

"No, Little Chick, I am not your husband. I might have been, had you not asked that question, but since you did, I am changing my seat to sit far, far away from you."

The Little Chick sighed and finished her teapot.

"Try an AA meeting," a sympathetic but indiscreet coworker suggested. "That's where I found my husband."

"*Are you my husband?*" she asked the fellow to her left at the AA meeting.

"That depends," he said, "on how low your self-esteem is."

As soon as they finished asking God, as they understood Him, for courage, serenity, and wisdom—in that exact order—the Little Chick backed out of the room, waving goodbye to her new friends.

But walking backward was almost as hard as fox-trotting. he fell down, and though she was fine, everyone agreed later that she was in denial.

"Doctors make good husbands," said one of the Little Chick's friends, who happened to be a doctor herself.

So the Little Chick scheduled an appointment with her eye doctor, who had a pleasant manner and no visible wedding ring. She found it romantic to sit in the dark with him as he gazed into her retinas with his powerful white light.

"Now, Little Chick," said the eye doctor in his soothing voice, "read the chart from top to bottom for me."

"$\mathcal{R}$, $\mathcal{U}$ . . ." the Little Chick read, and thought that the world was playing a cruel, cruel joke on her.

"Good, good," the eye doctor said, and then added, "You know, you have exactly the same astigmatism in your left eye that my girlfriend does. Weird."

"Baby," her best gay friend said to her, "come to this party on Saturday. There'll be lots of husbands there for you."

So she went, but all the cute ones flirted with her friend. "Sorry, baby," he said as he left with one of them. "I could have sworn some of them were going to be straight."

The Little Chick went to her high school reunion.

"Are you my husband?" she asked the former captain of the football team, whose divorce from the former secretary of the student council had just come through.

"No, Little Chip, I am not your husband," the former captain of the football team said, "though I think I did kinda like you once, for two weeks sophomore year. Here's my number if you want to migrate sometime."

The Little Chick went to get some punch.

"Are you my husband?" she asked the guy across the buffet table.

"No, Little Chick, I am not your husband. I still haven't forgiven you for turning me down for the prom all those years ago. Twist in the wind now, baby."

The Little Chick went to the gym. The ostrich next to her was reading a health-food magazine that showed that he, too, liked kelp, whole grains, and spring water. She thought he might be her soul mate.

"Are you my husband?" the Little Chick asked.

Oh, you're looking for a husband too?" the ostrich replied,
Aren't we all. It's hard, really hard. You might want to wear
something a little less bulky than those shorts—they really
emphasize your hips. Wow, check *him* out."

That night, the Little Chick had strange dreams:

"Are you my husband?"

"No, I am one of those folding paper things from sixth grade. Red, blue, green, or yellow? Pick one."

"Are you my husband?"

"No, I am a vibrator."

29

The Little Chick woke up with sweaty feathers. To clear he[r] head, she took a walk in the park, where she saw a cute young swan.

"Are you my husband?" she asked.

"No, Little Chick I am not your husband. I am the ugly duckling you used to baby-sit for! Do you want me to tell my mom you said hello?"

"AIEEEEEEEEEEEEEE!" squawked the Little Chick, and ran away from him as fast as her awkwardly jointed legs could take her.

The sky is falling, the Little Chick thought. I must
find a husband.

Down the street came a serious-looking platypus.

"Are you my husband?" she asked.
"No, Little Chick, I am not your husband. No one but a
platypus is going to raise my children, that's for damn sure."

"Little Chick," said one of her few remaining single friends, "embrace your singlehood. Freeze your eggs. Feed your head. Go on a cruise and sleep with some sleazy man."

The Little Chick considered this suggestion.

"Just be sure you use protection," her single friend, who knew about such things, added.

A cruise? The Little Chick looked at herself in the mirror and wished she'd lived in the seventies, when more people did things like that.

But she went on a cruise anyway.

She turned out to be a shuffleboard whiz.
All the old birds loved her . . .

. . . and on the last night she made out with the ship's purser, but then the cruise ended, and he sailed away, and she never found out exactly what it is that a purser does.

The Little Chick could feel her eggs aging. She could feel her biological clock tick tick ticking.

She went to visit her sister, who was married with a
little chick of her own.

"It's so great to see you," her sister said. "Hold her for me
for a minute, okay?" Then she left the room for three
hours to have an intense discussion with her husband
about family finances and their need for more alone time.

The Little Chick's niece, who was too young to know what she was doing, covered her aunt's new shirt with some corn mush that felt the need to go back up the way it had come down.

"Sorry," the Little Chick's sister said when she finally returned, "I must have lost track of the time." But the Little Chick could tell that she wasn't really sorry at all.

The Little Chick decided to go online.

One hundred and one males replied, most attaching high-resolution pictures that showed off their sleek feathers, bright irises, and smooth bills.

One of these must be my husband, thought the Little Chick, and she went out to meet some of them.

"I am not your husband," said the first date, "because I am already married. Is that an issue for you?"

"I might be your husband, at some point, in the due course of events," the second date said, "but first I'd like you to sign this agreement of mutual possible interest. It's pretty standard. . . ."

"I will be your husband," the third one said, "if you will pay my debt."

"U can be the showerhead," the last one said. "I will be the soap." But the Little Chick was not up on her Prince lyrics and failed this mysterious test.

The Little Chick went home and considered her life.

How could she be lonely, she thought,
with ninety-seven emails in her in-box?

But was she lonely?

It was difficult to say.

Not really, she thought.

Maybe she would never find a husband?

Maybe that wouldn't be the end of the world?

Maybe someday she would find a man she just wanted to b
with for a long time, possibly forever, and who wanted to b
with her for a long time, possibly forever, too?

And maybe sex with him would be really, really hot?

The Little Chick began to feel her feathers unruffle.

Overhead, the sky was clear blue and starry,
and as sturdy as sky can ever be.

Rachel Carpenter's nonfiction, humorous and otherwise, h. appeared in outlets as varied as *Martha Stewart Wedding* NPR, and mcsweeneys.net. Her fiction has run in sever literary magazines, including theatlantic.com and *One Stor* and has been read on the BBC. A native of Philadelphia, she currently at work on a novel. Learn more about her www.rachelcarpenter.com.

Sarah Bereczki is a Brooklyn-based illustrator/animator who clients include Oxygen Media, Nickelodeon, VH1, MT Planned Parenthood, and Soft Skull Press. She has create animated shorts, quizzes, and games for television and t web. She has also written and illustrated children's bool and comics. Samples of her work may be viewed www.itchygirl.com.